1996

MARY AND NIGEL

ANGLO-SAXON ARCHITECTURE

SHIRE ARCHAEOLOGY

Cover photograph
Earls Barton (Northamptonshire): the church tower.

Published by
SHIRE PUBLICATIONS LTD
Cromwell House, Church Street, Princes Risborough,
Aylesbury, Bucks, HP17 9AJ, UK.

Series Editor: James Dyer

ISBN 0 85263 570 2

First published 1983, reprinted 1989

Set in 11 point Times and printed in Great Britain by C. I. Thomas & Sons
(Haverfordwest) Ltd, Press Buildings, Merlins Bridge, Haverfordwest.

Contents

List of illustrations

Preface

This book is concerned primarily with stone buildings which survive from the long period between the end of the Roman occupation of England during the fifth century and the Norman Conquest in the eleventh. The story of Anglo-Saxon architecture begins with the importation into England of a new kind of building by Christian missionaries during the sixth and seventh centuries. Before this time, the pagan Anglo-Saxons had built exclusively in timber and apparently regarded the ruins of Roman masonry buildings with superstitious awe as 'the work of giants'. Timber construction continued after the reintroduction of stone and many major buildings were made of wood right up to the Norman Conquest.

The missionaries who brought the new styles of building came from Italy and Gaul, where the classical legacy was still strong. Along with writing, painting and sculpture, the art of building in stone — architecture — had not been forgotten after the fall of Rome. The missionaries came to convert the English, but they also brought with them a package of new ideas which was to revolutionise Anglo-Saxon culture and society. The church, which never lost its broader European perspective, became a major engine of civilisation; Anglo-Saxon architecture merely reflects this great influence.

It is no accident that virtually all the Anglo-Saxon stone buildings which we know of are churches. It was Latin Christianity which reintroduced the technology of stone construction, and the church itself was the major consumer of the new techniques. The cost and complexity of stone construction were normally reserved for the ultimate purpose, the reverence of God.

Key to symbols used on church plans

N = nave
A = apse
C = chancel
T = tower

P = porticus
n = narthex
a = aisle

Fig. 1. The Anglian Tower, York; the dating of the tower is uncertain, but it presumably belongs to the period between the seventh and ninth centuries when York was the political capital of Northumbria.

Fig. 2. St John's church at Escomb, built of reused stones from the Roman fort at Binchester. The south porch is added, and the crow-step gables are later, but the overall proportions of the building are unchanged.

1
The nature of the evidence

The greatest problem which confronts the student of Anglo-Saxon architecture is the partiality of the surviving evidence. It is as if he is being asked to complete a jigsaw, having been told in advance that half of the most useful pieces have been thrown away. No first rank church or secular building has come down to us, no cathedral or royal palace, or even nobleman's hall. The sum of the evidence amounts to four hundred or so churches scattered across England which contain greater or lesser proportions of Anglo-Saxon fabric. With the quirkish exception of the so-called 'Anglian Tower' at York (fig. 1), no secular buildings survive at all. Similarly, apart from Escomb (Durham) (fig. 2), Bradford-on-Avon (Wiltshire) and a handful of others, none of the churches is well preserved.

In the face of such evidence, it is hardly surprising that what remains often fails to make much sense. Various scholars have devised developmental sequences ever since the recognition of Anglo-Saxon architecture by Thomas Rickman early in the nineteenth century, but none has been found totally satisfactory. The most that can be reliably said is that there exist certain styles and features which are of undoubted Anglo-Saxon manufacture, and that they differ widely in scale, elaboration and to some extent in date according to the importance of the structures in which they appear.

There are certain features which are useful in discriminating between periods; their exclusive appearance in buildings which are 'early', 'middle' or 'late', or a combination of them, serves as a basic dating framework. Different types of window openings appear to have chronological significance, for example. Single-splayed megalithic lights are present in the early Northumbrian churches (fig. 23a), and since they have not been found in definite ninth-century or later contexts they are held to be 'early'. Single-splayed lights with through-stones, on the other hand, are known in both the early and latest periods and accordingly have no chronological significance. Conversely, double-splayed windows are unknown from the early period and hence are indicative of a later date.

Long-and-short quoins, pilaster strips, hoodmouldings and stripwork all have their earliest appearance on the tower at Barnack (Cambridgeshire), which is perhaps of later ninth-century date. After this, they continue in use to the end of the period and are not uncommon in Saxo-Norman contexts. This pattern is closely followed by belfry towers with their distinctive openings; none is known before the ninth century, and most appear substantially later.

Such limited certainty is a product of the evidence, for not only do relatively few Anglo-Saxon churches survive, but also they tend not to be the best examples for our purpose. Most of the best preserved churches are in remote and therefore 'unfashionable' places from the viewpoints of architectural style and elaboration. The great centres of innovation and development, such as Winchester, Canterbury, Hexham and London, show little physical evidence of their Anglo-Saxon primacy beyond a few excavated ground plans and architectural fragments. Hence it is very difficult to use the normal art historical methods of tracing the introduction of a style or technique and its gradual diffusion outwards from its point of origin. Rather we have many sites which were in receipt of architectural and artistic influences at second or third hand. Thus we are confronted with an admixture of styles in most places, and the very reasons which led to the survival of the evidence, i.e. remoteness and political insignificance, also mean that they are least representative of the Anglo-Saxon architectural achievement.

We have only to contrast the richness and variety of the Norman architectural heritage with the Anglo-Saxon. Where are the Saxon cathedrals, the monasteries, the major churches and parish churches? The causes of this phenomenon are, in part, easy to see. After the Norman Conquest, there was apparently a desire on the part of the conquerors to eradicate 'Englishness'; thus most major buildings were rebuilt in new and foreign styles. Similarly in the case of Anglo-Saxon sculpture; time and again we read nineteenth-century accounts of stone crosses and tombs being recovered from Norman foundation trenches during restorations. The wholesale demolition of Saxon buildings and the throwing down of their sculpture indicate a systematic attempt to erase the 'English' style. If this were not so, we would expect Saxon and Norman buildings to survive today in roughly equal numbers, since later ages would presumably have dealt fairly evenly with both.

A further factor relating to the surviving Saxon churches is their uneven chronological distribution. From the earliest period, i.e. from *c* 600 to the time of the Danish raids in 800, come 14 per cent of the survivors. The troubled times between 800 and 950 provide only 3 per cent of the total, whilst the latest period, 950 to 1100, can show a massive 83 per cent, although this figure must include an uncertain number of 'Saxo-Norman' churches built either immediately before or after the Conquest.

These percentages reflect changes in church foundation as much as straightforward survival. The Danish raids had a devastating effect on the church, and there must have been a great hiatus in church building for that reason alone. But beyond this, there are important differences between the pre- and post-Danish ages. During the early period, most churches were monastic 'minster' churches, which sent out priests over a wide area to minister to the laity. At that time, parish churches were virtually unknown, and the only lesser churches would have been on royal estates or other high-ranking settlements. Local communities in the converted parts of the country would have assembled at fenced-off open-air preaching places. Here they would listen to the word of God preached by the visiting minster clergy, perhaps gathering round a cross of wood or stone which marked the place.

By the tenth century the picture had changed, and during the reign of Ethelred II there existed a system of churches which ranged from 'head minsters' (i.e. cathedrals) at one end of the spectrum through lesser churches with graveyards to 'field churches' or country chapels at the other. The minsters also carried on. This increase in the types of churches is reflected by the increased number of surviving buildings, most of which belong to the category of 'lesser churches with graveyards', which are the parish churches. This type of church was founded extensively by noblemen both for their own convenience and also through genuine piety. It is accordingly unsurprising that most of our churches come from later Saxon times.

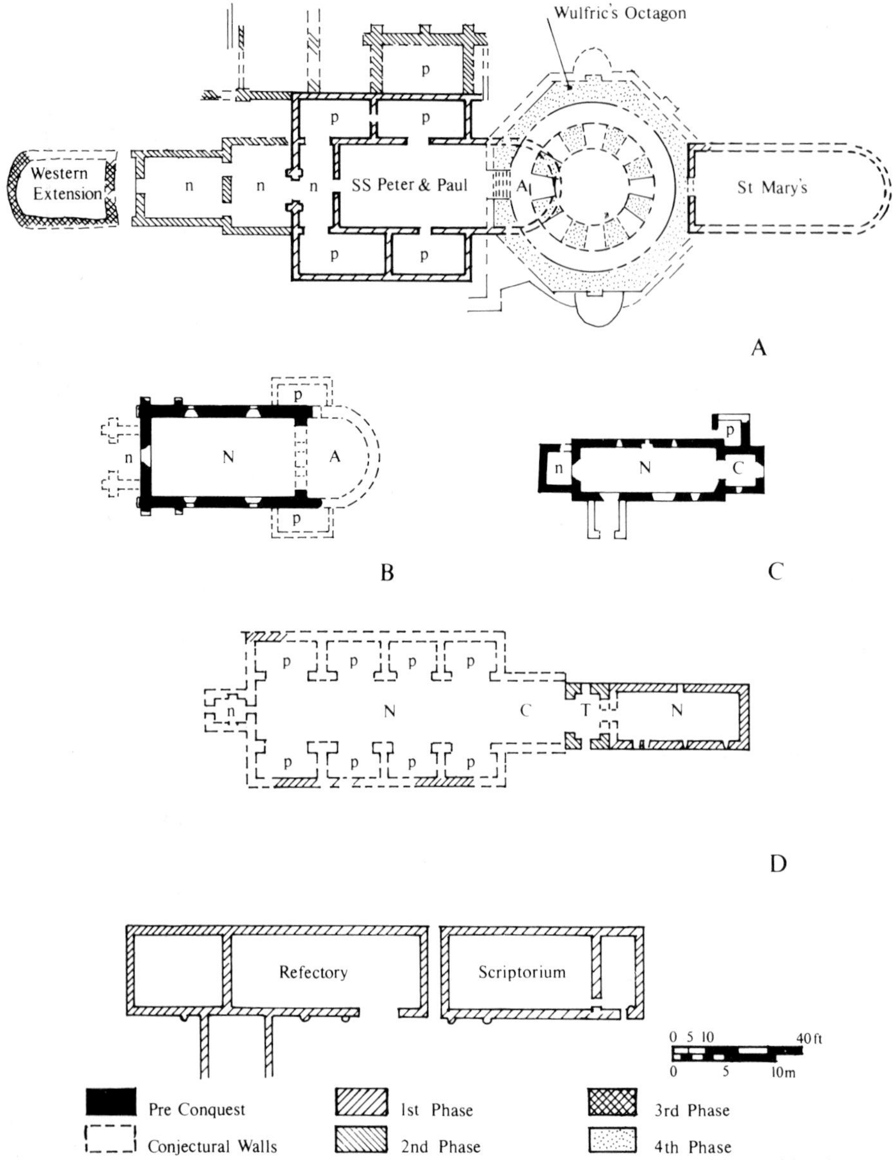

Fig. 3. A The monastic church of St Peter and St Paul at Canterbury, with Wulfric's later octagon linking it to St Mary's church to the east. The western apse recalls St Oswald's Priory, Gloucester (after Saunders). **B** Bradwell-on-Sea (after Taylor). **C** Escomb (after Pocock and Wheeler). **D** Jarrow, showing what were perhaps two churches set end to end originally with the claustral buildings below (after Cramp).

2
Form and function

As we have seen, it was the influence of Latin Christianity which brought about the introduction of stone architecture into Anglo-Saxon England. The earliest stone churches are to be found in Kent and Essex and are directly attributable to the success of the conversion effected by St Augustine after his arrival in 597. At least seven churches were built in the kingdom of Kent itself by St Augustine and his followers, with an outlier at Bradwell-on-Sea in Essex. These 'Kentish' churches form a discrete group, and their details foreshadow many of the main features of Anglo-Saxon liturgical planning.

The basic plan form of the Kentish churches comprised two elements: a rectangular nave for the laity and altar, with a smaller apsidal chapel to the east for the use of the clergy. The two spaces were normally divided by a screen of three arches, an arrangement which can still be seen in the upstanding east wall of the church at Bradwell. The two-cell plan has parallels in North Africa and round the Mediterranean; there were almost certainly European examples closer at hand, but they have not yet been discovered. The nave and sanctuary plan with the emphasis on the east end of the building was the basis of most later churches, though some late Saxon churches diverged from it by making the west end a liturgical feature in its own right.

At the monastic church of St Peter and St Paul in Canterbury, which is the earliest of the Kentish group, being under construction when St Augustine died in 604, we can see several changes in the two-cell plan (fig. 3A). In particular, the provision of a western porch or *narthex* foreshadows later Saxon interest in the western parts of churches. Although the basic function of the narthex seems to have been to act as an antechamber to the nave, it is probable that it was used for baptisms and as a place for withdrawal of penitents, since it was outside the liturgical plan proper.

This idea of an adjunct to the main liturgical space probably applied to the second development of the two-cell plan, which was the addition of small lateral chambers to the north and south of the nave and chancel. Such chambers are called *porticus* (both singular and plural) in the early documents and were to become a distinctive feature of early church planning. That they were not considered as part of the plan proper is suggested by their use as mortuary chapels. Before the Synod of Mainz in 813 burials were forbidden inside churches, yet at Canterbury and elsewhere porticus were the burial places of important lay and ecclesiastical people from the first. Indeed, Augustine himself was buried in the north porticus of the abbey church of St Peter and St Paul.

In some instances porticus overlap the junction between nave and chancel (fig. 3B). This suggests that, where there are chambers to north and south, they may have acted as prothesis and diaconicon, as in the eastern church. If this was so, then the northern chamber would have been used for the preparation of the host and for offerings, whilst the southern would have housed books and vessels as well as serving as a vestry.

Later evidence suggests that an even wider range of functions was fulfilled by porticus. Documentary accounts of the great church of the Holy Wisdom at York mention 'many porticus', and references to *solaria* or upper chambers remind us that porticus, like the naves of Anglo-Saxon churches, could rise through two storeys. The York description also records the existence of thirty altars — a prodigious number, which is only explicable if the porticus were used as the sites of subsidiary altars. Porticus may also have served as baptistries, as galleries for lay persons at major festivals, and possibly as 'courtrooms' for judicial sessions. This last function has been suggested for the later tower chamber at Barnack.

The second group of early stone churches was established in Northumbria after the Synod of Whitby in 663, when the Roman church overcame the Celtic. Until that time the Celtic church had built largely in wood, and it was only afterwards that stone buildings became common. Two churches in particular, at Monkwearmouth and Jarrow (Tyne and Wear), stand as memorials to the new initiative in the north. They were built by St Benedict Biscop, a young Northumbrian noble churchman who had returned from Europe fired by the sights he had seen there. He set about imitating these architectural triumphs by importing not merely the building technology, but also the craftsmen to do the job.

In the Venerable Bede's *History of the English Church and People* we learn of Biscop's great building project, the 'double monastery' of St Peter and St Paul on what we would today call a 'split site'. The first part of the monastery was built at Wearmouth (now called Monkwearmouth) in the years after 674; he then built the linked house at Jarrow after a grant of land for the purpose from King Ecgfrith in 681. Bede tells us that Biscop went to Gaul to seek masons to build him a church of stone in the Roman manner. Later, he sent word to Gaul that he required the services of glaziers to add the finishing touches to his new buildings. The monasteries must have inspired great wonder in the minds of the Northumbrians.

Benedict Biscop's buildings were, like the Kentish churches, very well constructed with mortar floors, plastered walls, glazed windows and leaded roofs, all in the best European taste. Both sites have been extensively remodelled but each had at least two churches; this idea of 'families' of churches on a particular site is an important feature of liturgical planning, which had appeared before at Canterbury (fig. 3A). The northern monastic churches were probably basilican in plan, as at Jarrow, and had flanking porticus (fig. 3D). However, the Northumbrian churches, with the exception of the easternmost projection at Hexham (Northumberland), had square-ended chancels from the first, as opposed to the apsidal terminations used in the Kentish group. This feature, together with the longer and narrower proportions of the naves of the early northern churches, has led to suggestions of Celtic constructional influence arising from timber construction. At Monkwearmouth there is a handsome two-storey western porch (fig. 11), which retains much of its original decoration.

Excavations at Monkwearmouth and Jarrow have revealed traces of the conventual buildings. The plans vary between the two sites, but both had some substantial stone buildings with plastered walls and glazed windows. At Jarrow two major buildings were found, both rectangular in plan with subdivisions. The western building may have been a refectory, and fragments of a decorated stone shaft with a heavy sandstone base have been interpreted as a lectern; this would accord with the known practice of reading scripture to the monks during meals. The second building at Jarrow resembles a secular hall in its plan; it consisted of a larger public space, in this case used for reading and writing, with a smaller room partitioned off at the east end for the use of the abbot or a senior monk. Subsidiary wattle huts were found near the main buildings. Apparently they were used for industrial activities, a relationship which is again reminiscent of secular planning.

Benedict Biscop's initiative was soon taken up by another great churchman, St Wilfrid. He built splendid churches at Hexham, Ripon and York which were evidently even more ambitious than those which had gone before. Sadly, nothing is known of the church at York, and little remains of the other two apart from incomplete plans. We know that Hexham was a basilican building with many columns and porticus, and that it possessed such refinements as first-floor galleries and an underfloor crypt. These innovations were doubtless a result of Wilfrid's extensive continental travels; the crypt at Hexham is closely similar to that at Ripon and this similarity attests their common origins. The crypts were probably built to house holy relics which Wilfrid's chronicler Eddius tells us he had brought back from Rome. They were planned with two entrances in order that pilgrims might file past the relic chambers and venerate the contents.

But seventh-century Northumbria had lesser as well as greater churches. At Escomb (Durham) is a small church with a simple nave and chancel plan with evidence for a northern porticus and a western annexe. The chancel is square-ended, and the whole building is only a little over 50 feet (15 m) long (fig. 3C). Nothing is known of the circumstances of the foundation of St John's church at Escomb, but its early date is undisputed, and its existence indicates that church building had begun to spread outwards from the primary monastic centres.

Most of the smaller early churches probably followed the simple cellular plan seen at Escomb, a pattern which was to remain in use until the end of our period. The basic elements of a nave and chancel, whether square or apsidal-ended, with a western narthex and flanking porticus were the common currency of church building. Excavation of the Old Minster at Winchester, where the Anglo-Saxon Chronicle records that King Cenwalh completed a church in 648, has shown that the earliest phase, presumably his church, had a familiar plan of nave, chancel and porticus (fig. 4B). The altar was at the east end of the nave and the north porticus contained a well. An unusual feature of the site was the survival of some stone paving stones in the chancel.

But whilst a simple cellular plan may have been the most common amongst the early churches, more complex structures are known. Apart from the basilican churches at Hexham and Jarrow, All Saints' church at Brixworth (Northamptonshire) is a large and imposing basilican building on a grand scale; here there is none of the simplicity of Escomb. A broad nave with continuous flanking porticus was entered through a western porch. The porticus opened into the nave through large, though relatively narrow, arches. The presbytery, which is the same width as the nave, now terminates in a later polygonal sanctuary

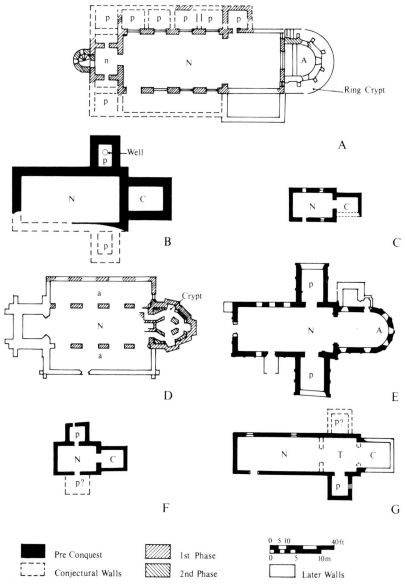

Fig. 4. A Brixworth (after Taylor). **B** The earliest church on the site of the Old Minster at Winchester, excavated plan (after Taylor). **C** Odda's Chapel, Deerhurst (after Taylor). **D** Wing, showing subterranean crypt (after Taylor). **E** Worth (after Taylor). **F** St Laurence's Chapel, Bradford-on-Avon (after Clapham). **G** Breamore (after Taylor).

with ring crypt (fig. 4A). Although the dating of Brixworth to the seventh century has been disputed, it is almost certainly an 'early' church, and its magnificence is consonant with its identification as 'Clofesho', a monastery which was the site of several important synods.

The later Saxon period, from around 850 onwards, saw considerable changes in church architecture, and some very elaborate buildings are known. But not all later churches were large and complex. Two of the latest and most closely dated, Odda's Chapel at Deerhurst (Gloucestershire, fig. 4C) and St Gregory's at Kirkdale (North Yorkshire), which can be placed in the decade or so before the Conquest, have simple nave and chancel plans which would not have been out of place in the seventh century. Clearly, simplicity of plan is no automatic index of antiquity. The cellular plan continued, and its influence is plain even in many larger churches.

One of the main concepts relevant to later churches is the 'additive' as opposed to the 'integrated' plan. This means that many of the greater churches were not built originally on a large scale, but that they grew out of small existing churches by the simple expedient of adding further cells or porticus.

Perhaps the clearest example of such a development is the monastic church of St Mary's at Deerhurst (Gloucestershire). Here, a combined programme of structural analysis and archaeological excavation has provided a remarkable picture of both the addition and subtraction of cells, for the process could be reversed if required. There were six main phases in the pre-Conquest building (fig. 5) and they showed not only horizontal but also vertical development, since both nave and at least the principal porticus appear to have had upper storeys.

The first church at Deerhurst was a simple rectangle with a porch at the west end. A semicircular apse was added to the east, followed by the construction of two flanking porticus to the north and south. Next it seems that the church was raised, since the upper parts of the nave and side chapels appear to be secondary to the lower parts; this is partly indicated by the occurrence of herringbone work only in the upper walls. We must therefore imagine a 'double decker' church with activities going on at two levels. Later still, the western tower was built, the easternmost chapels were demolished, and the semicircular apse was replaced by a polygonal structure decorated externally by panelling outlined by pilaster strips. Finally, the side chapels were extended westwards to provide a whole row of small chambers.

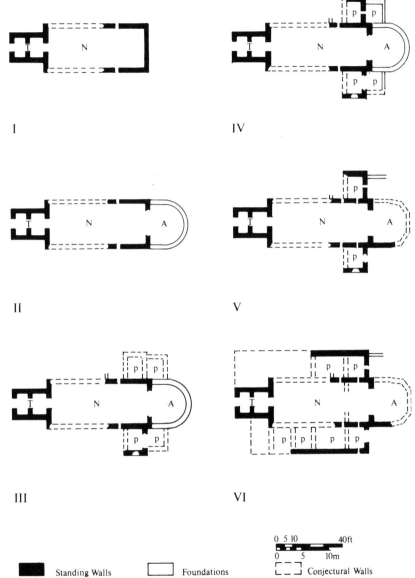

Standing Walls   Foundations   L _ _ J Conjectural Walls

Fig. 5. Deerhurst phase plans. **I** Simple two-cell church. **II** Addition of apse. **III** Flanking porticus added to east end. **IV** Structure raised. **V** Easternmost porticus demolished and rounded apse replaced by polygonal structure. **VI** Porticus extended westwards (after Taylor).

Deerhurst provides a clear pattern of successive changes in the fabric of a church which eventually culminated in a large and impressive structure. Internally, however, there would have been little impression of size; the nave roof would have seemed low, and the porticus no more than side rooms opening off the main space through narrow doorways. There was no major integrated central space in the manner of later aisled plans.

The liturgical uses of such a church must have differed from later practices therefore, with separate functions being carried out in specially reserved places away from the main body of the plan. This feeling of 'reserve' irresistibly reminds us of monastic cells, which were distinct from the main traffic of their sites. It has indeed been suggested that the upper storey of the nave at Deerhurst might have served as a monastic dormitory. Perhaps this is a clue to a different type of monasticism, in which the plan centred on the church itself, rather than being arranged in the more normal claustral buildings which the Northumbrian sites of Monkwearmouth and Jarrow possessed.

That there was another, parallel line of church development is suggested by the comparatively early occurrence of integrated plans. At Brixworth, for example, the basic basilican plan of broad nave and flanking porticus was laid out simultaneously. Whilst the Brixworth plan is thus of a single phase rather than being additive it is not yet an architecturally integrated church, because the porticus were still physically distanced from the nave by their small doorways.

At Wing (Buckinghamshire), however, we see a second stage in this process (fig. 4D). The dating of Wing is disputed, but the basic nave and chancel could, like Brixworth, be as early as the seventh century. Here the nave walls are relatively insubstantial and are pierced by wider arches which opened either into porticus or even into full-blown aisles. The balance of the elements has changed here; instead of the solid walls being dominant, the arches are wider, and a much more open type of plan was plainly intended. At Wing we can perhaps see the beginnings of the truly integrated church in which all the elements of the plan centred on the main space.

One of the most distinctive features of later Saxon liturgical planning was, however, its diversity. No one type of church predominated, unless we go right down the scale to the simple nave and chancel plan with or without a western tower. Instead, there is a range of plans and styles of building, each of which doubtless fulfilled particular functions, and which had different

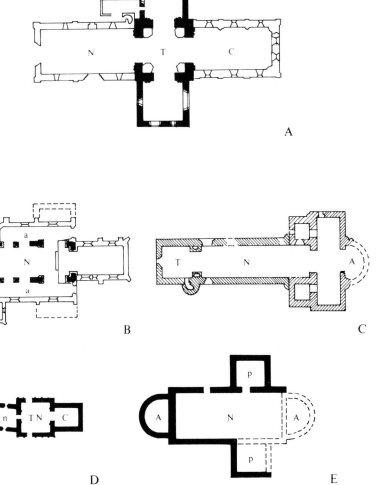

Fig. 6. A Stow (after Taylor). **B** Great Paxton (after Clapham). **C** North Elmham (after Rigold). **D** Barton-upon-Humber (after Rodwell). **E** St Oswald's Priory, Gloucester (after Heighway).

patrons and designers and therefore different influences acting upon them.

Some like Worth (West Sussex, fig. 4E) and Bradford-on-Avon (Wiltshire, fig. 4F), still consisted basically of two cells with porticus added to north and south. At Worth the porticus are sited well to the east end of the nave and have relatively wide arches into them; here we see the beginning of transepts, and hence of the cruciform plan, whether by accident or design. This early arrangement is distinguished from later medieval cruciform churches on the basis that the transepts are lower than the nave, 'low transepts', unlike later transepts, which are generally of equal height. At Breamore (Hampshire, fig. 4G) and Milborne Port (Somerset) we see a similar development, but here the crossing is emphasised by the addition of a central tower. At Stow (Lincolnshire), however, transepts seem to have existed which stood to the full height of the nave walls (fig. 6A).

At Great Paxton (Cambridgeshire) a further line of development harks back to the nascent aisled plan seen at Wing (fig. 6B). Whereas the churches mentioned above have transepts, whether low or full, Great Paxton is remarkable in having both low transepts as well as proper nave arcades opening into continuous aisles. The manor of Paxton was held by Edward the Confessor, and the church there was almost certainly built by him; royal patronage is precisely the milieu from which we would expect such an advanced design to have come.

The so-called cathedral church at North Elmham (Norfolk) demonstrates a further development in transeptal planning in which a compartment runs across the whole width of the building immediately west of the apse forming a 'continuous transept' (fig. 6C). This plan form is unusual in England, and its introduction, perhaps from the Mediterranean, attests the patronage which major churches could command.

A further indication of wealthy patronage was the provision of crypts in churches. The reliquary crypts at Hexham and Ripon have been mentioned. To these can be added further examples of larger chambers intended for public access, such as Wing (fig. 7A). There are two other types which are rather different, however. The first of these is the ring crypt, as at Brixworth (fig. 4A), which was intended for the passage of pilgrims, but in this case they were conducted into a narrow passage for circulation past a small relic chamber, rather than gaining access to a single larger space.

The third type of crypt was not originally intended for public

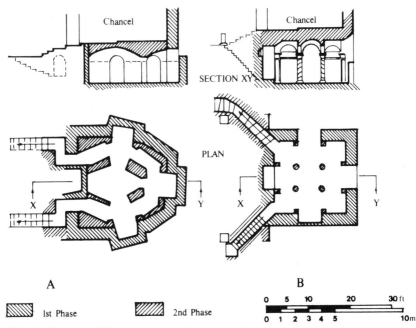

Fig. 7. Crypts. **A** Wing. **B** Repton (after Taylor).

access: this was the simple burial chamber. The most celebrated example of this class of structure is the crypt of St Wystan's church at Repton (Derbyshire, fig. 7B). Here, a small square chamber was built on the floor of a large hole dug for the purpose, the hole was backfilled, and the crypt was probably reserved as the burial place of the Mercian kings, amongst whom was Saint Wystan. When Wystan's cult grew in popularity, access to the chamber proved inadequate and two staircases were cut into the west wall of the structure, in the manner of Hexham and Ripon. A smaller, unmolested burial chamber was found during the excavations at Glastonbury Abbey; this has been interpreted as the resting place of King Ine.

Yet another style of later church is represented by the immense tower naves at Barton-upon-Humber (Humberside, fig. 6D) and Earls Barton (Northamptonshire). Although late in date, these churches show little regard for the integrated plan. At Barton-upon-Humber the structure consisted of a larger central tower nave with a baptistry to the west and a chancel to the east. The rooms opened into one another through relatively narrow doors, and the atmosphere would have been almost claustrophobic, particularly since there were upper floors in both the east and west rooms, and a gallery projected into the central nave space.

Church towers generally appear to have been a late Saxon innovation, possibly influenced by Italian campanili. Their development is perhaps merely the last stage of a sequence of elaboration of the western ends of churches which reaches back to the western porches at Monkwearmouth and elsewhere. At Ledsham (West Yorkshire) there was a two-storeyed western annexe, but instead of the entry into the church being in the west wall it was in the south side of the annexe; at Escomb there was an annexe, but apparently without any door into the church. Plainly we must not see these western projections merely as 'porches' and nothing more. Recent excavations at St Oswald's Priory at Gloucester (fig. 6E) have taken the story a little further by revealing a western apse, presumably balancing one to the east, though this is unknown as yet. Here we have clear evidence of a bifocal plan where both the east and west ends of the church had liturgical as well as structural emphasis as at Canterbury (fig. 3A).

The most developed form of this idea was the so-called 'westwork', a term coined by the Germans to describe the complex structural elaboration of the western parts of early churches. In England, such westworks have long been suspected. An early and hotly debated account of the Saxon cathedral at Canterbury appears to describe a western sanctuary which might have been housed in such a structure. But recently, in the excavations of the Old Minster at Winchester, and at Sherborne (Dorset, fig. 8) and in the standing western fabric at St Mary's, Deerhurst, we can begin to see the insular echo of the full majesty of such continental exemplars as Corvey in West Germany and Centula St Riquier near Abbeville.

Amongst the functions fulfilled by westworks were the housing of subsidiary altars, the provision of galleries for choirs of 'angels' or for prominent laymen, the siting of judicial courts, the housing of bells, their use as treasuries and the straightforward task of giving access to the upper levels of churches.

When we consider the seemingly more prosaic Anglo-Saxon tower, we can, for western towers at least, detect some of the functional and ritual significance of westworks in them. The idea that towers were merely for supporting belfries does not explain

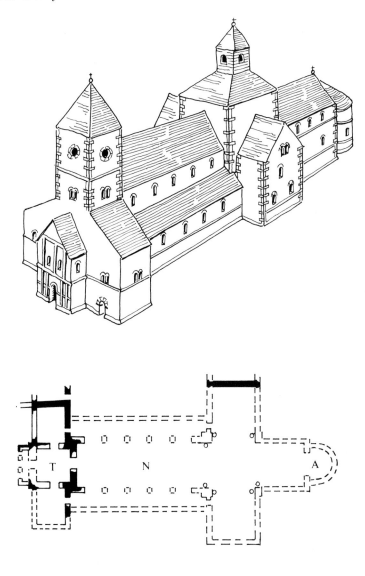

Fig. 8. Reconstruction drawing and plan of Sherborne Abbey; note the elaboration of the west end (after Gibbs and Taylor).

their complexity. If simple access to upper storeys of the church was all that was required of towers, their floor areas could be much less, and the existence of separate stair turrets at such sites as Hough-on-the-Hill (Lincolnshire, fig. 9) and Brixworth would be rendered unnecessary.

In many towers there are doorways which open from the upper floors into thin air, with no possibility of an external stair or floor ever having been present, as at Earls Barton (fig. 28). It is possible that they link with the use of towers as treasuries, a practice attested at Peterborough in 1070. If precious relics or banners were kept in the tower, such doorways might have been useful places from which to display them to the faithful on feast days. Apart from the doorways, the large floor areas of some tower chambers, together with the existence of cupboards in their walls, suggest that they may have been dwellings, either for the clergy or for a deacon. At Deerhurst and Bosham (West Sussex) there were almost certainly first-floor chapels in the towers, and at Wing, Tredington (Warwickshire) and Stoke d'Abernon (Surrey) there were galleries attached to the west walls of the nave.

The dating of towers depends upon differing views of their origins. If they are seen as deriving from Italian campanili, which were basically bell towers, then they cannot occur in England before the tenth century. If, however, we are persuaded that they develop out of the general westwork tradition, then an earlier date is quite feasible; the tower at Barnack, one of the most elaborate, has been dated to the ninth century, for example. Whatever their starting date, towers proved very popular in England, and just under one hundred are known, the majority of which are western towers. The design of towers and of their characteristic belfry openings affords a rare opportunity to identify local schools of Anglo-Saxon building. Three major groups are known:

The Lincolnshire Group. This consists of fifteen examples, mostly in the old county of Lincolnshire. They have a tall, gaunt appearance and are undecorated apart from the belfry lights. They normally have only two external stages (fig. 10).

The Northumbrian Group. There are six examples, all in the old kingdom of Northumbria. They share the tall plainness of the

Fig. 9 (right). Western stair turret at Hough-on-the-Hill (Lincolnshire).

156,916

Fig. 10. Lincolnshire towers: *(top left)* Rothwell; *(top right)* St Mary-le-Wigford, Lincoln; *(left)* St Peter's, Lincoln.

Fig. 11. Northumbrian towers: *(top left)* Monkwearmouth — the seventh-century timber porch occupied the bottom two storeys; *(top right)* St Andrew's, Bywell; *(right)* Ovingham (Northumberland). The stripwork surrounds of the belfry lights and the circular sounding holes can be seen in the topmost stages of the towers.

Fig. 12. East Anglian flint towers: *(top left)* Newton-by-Castleacre; *(top right)* Great Dunham; *(left)* Haddiscoe Thorpe — the topmost belfry stage is Norman (photograph by Peter Warner).

Lincolnshire Group, but their belfry lights have distinctive stripwork around them with or without round sound holes (fig. 11).

The East Anglian Towers. This is perhaps the most controversial 'group' and is made up of round towers. Most such towers (there are twenty-one altogether) occur in Norfolk and Suffolk, and it has been suggested that they represent a local design response to a shortage of good freestone for building, since they did not require quoins in their construction. However, freestone is used in some of them, and square towers could also be built out of the local flint, as Newton-by-Castleacre (Norfolk) reminds us. But why a particular design should prove so popular in such a restricted area without such a practical explanation is difficult to fathom (fig. 12).

Other 'groups' are even less satisfactory. The so-called Midland Group includes the major stripwork decorated towers. The Rhenish Helm Group refers to the surviving example at Sompting, together with the vestigial evidence at Cambridge St Benet's and, perhaps, Flixton (Suffolk).

Fig. 13. Reused Roman stones in St Wilfrid's crypt at Hexham.

3
Building materials

Many of the first Anglo-Saxon stone churches were constructed from reused Roman materials which were locally available on their sites. The Kentish churches used stone, bricks and tiles from the nearby sites of a Roman town in the case of Canterbury, and of Saxon Shore forts at Reculver and elsewhere. Indeed, it seems possible that these early church sites were selected because of their proximity to handy 'quarries' of materials, although the ruined walls of the forts in particular would have formed ideal monastic enclosures dividing the religious within from the profane without. This picture of reuse is also true of some of the Northumbrian group of churches. Wilfrid reused material from the Hadrian's Wall fort of *Corstopitum* in his crypt at Hexham (fig. 13), and Escomb church (Durham) was largely built of stones from nearby Binchester.

It is not known precisely when stone quarrying began in Anglo-Saxon England, but the occurrence of monolithic stone crosses from the seventh century onwards suggests that the organised winning of stone had begun quite early. Architecturally, it is clear that quarrying began on at least a small scale by the late eighth century, as the 18 foot (5.5 m) long sections of friezework at Breedon-on-the-Hill (Leicestershire) indicate (fig. 30g). By the late Saxon period, freestone of good quality from such quarries as Barnack (Cambridgeshire, fig. 15) and Box (Wiltshire) was carried a distance of as much as 70 miles (110 km). The use of high quality stone for architectural sculpture and other specialised purposes suggests considerable skill in selecting and working stone beds, and this probably included deep quarrying.

Saxon mortar was generally very durable, and different mixes were employed for walls and floors. Floors with a top coating of brick or tile dust in the manner of Roman *opus signinum* are recorded from the early churches in particular. Later 'mortar' floors may in some cases merely represent the bedding for robbed paving slabs of the sort found at the Old Minster at Winchester.

Tough walling mortars enabled the Saxons to build their characteristically tall and thin walls, many of which were less than 3 feet (0.9 m) wide. At Brixworth (Northamptonshire), analysis of the mortar has shown that average particle size was closely similar to that used in modern mixes, suggesting that the

Fig. 14. An impression of one of the Northampton mortar mixers (after Williams).

preparation of mortar was a skilled undertaking. This impression is strengthened by evidence from an excavation near St Peter's church in Northampton which revealed the remains of three mechanical mixers, which probably required at least four men each to drive them. The mixers probably dated from the ninth century and provide remarkable evidence of the level of

Fig. 15. The 'Hills and Holes' at Barnack, caused by stone quarrying over many centuries.

organisation of the Anglo-Saxon building industry at a relatively early date (fig. 14).

Plaster was used extensively both inside and outside Saxon churches, as well as for carved and moulded stucco work. Plastered and painted stones from the excavations at Winchester complement the remarkable paintings at Nether Wallop (Hampshire). Elsewhere, the evidence for plaster is mostly indirect, as at Avebury (Wiltshire) and Bibury (Gloucestershire) where drilled holes for lath supports round circular windows attest its former existence (see fig. 24). Externally, the rebated quoins at Wittering (Cambridgeshire) were doubtless designed to accommodate plaster (fig. 22). Similarly relief stripwork schemes were probably intended to be seen against smooth plastered panels (fig. 28). Plastered stones have been excavated at Repton (Derbyshire) and plastered tomb interiors have also been discovered there. At Monkwearmouth (Tyne and Wear) pinkish plaster is reported from both the early church and the conventual buildings. Stucco work can be seen on the crossing capitals at Milborne Port (Somerset) (though this could be a nineteenth-century restoration). Stucco presumably also existed on the now flat carving of the Virgin at Deerhurst, and its presence is suspected on the incomplete Christ in Majesty at Barton-upon-Humber.

Window glass is known from a number of churches, though most has come from important monastic sites. Hundreds of fragments were found at Monkwearmouth and Jarrow, mostly coloured green, but with some shades of yellow, blue, brown and red streaked with green. Whilst this glass is presumably the product of Benedict Biscop's Gaulish glaziers, finds from as far apart as Repton and Winchester suggest the later existence of an English glass industry, an observation confirmed for the tenth century by the discovery of a glass workshop at Glastonbury Abbey (Somerset). Finds of window glass in the excavations at

Fig. 16. Hogback tombstone from Brompton (North Yorkshire) showing a stylised 'house' with a roof made from triangular (?wooden) shingles.

Fig. 17. Arch at Brixworth using 'Roman' bricks.

Fig. 18 *(below).* The central tower at Breamore.

Fig. 19. A simplified diagram of the timbering of the 'helmed' roof at Sompting (after Hewett).

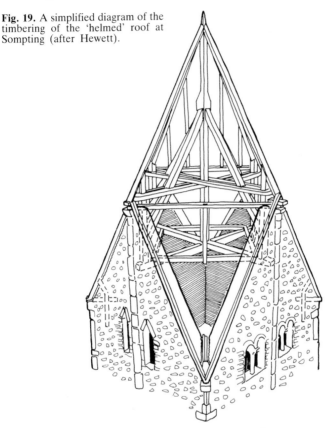

Escomb suggest that some lesser churches were glazed.

Roofs were presumably mainly of thatch since little other evidence has been found. Small triangular wooden shingles are probably depicted in some manuscript illustrations and stone carvings (fig. 16) and are known from the Winchester excavations. At Monkwearmouth thin limestone slates were used in conjunction with lead flashings in the Roman style. Lead was probably widely used in sheet form by late Saxon times for the roofs of important churches, and as early as 801 Alcuin donated tin for a special roof at York.

As far as is known, the Saxons did not manufacture roof or floor tiles in fired clay after the Roman fashion, and any fired clay bricks found in Anglo-Saxon structures were thought to have been reused Roman material. At Brixworth however, where

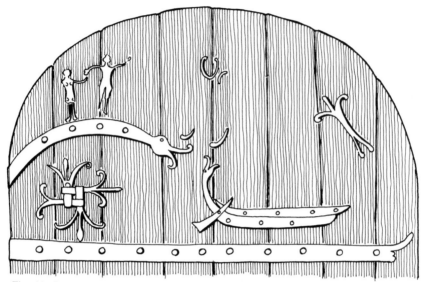

Fig. 20. Iron door furniture at Stillingfleet (North Yorkshire).

large numbers of 'Roman' bricks are used in the fabric of the early church (fig. 17), thermoluminescent determinations suggest that some of them could be of Anglo-Saxon date. This possibility is reinforced by sites such as Britford (Wiltshire), where regular fired clay tiles appear as integral elements in a very precise architectural composition (fig. 30f).

Wood was a basic structural material in its own right but was extensively used in stone churches as well. Roofs must have used tons of prime timber, and it is thought that the basic structure of the famous 'helmed' tower roof at Sompting (West Sussex) is Saxon (fig. 19). The central wooden tower at Breamore (Hampshire) probably follows the original very closely, though no part of the existing work is Saxon (fig. 18). Some church doors, notably at Buttsbury and Hadstock (both in Essex), show distinctive constructional features which have been identified as Anglo-Saxon, and at Earls Barton (Northamptonshire) there are two ladders which may have provided access to the tower there for over a thousand years. Finally, the iron fittings on some church doors have been claimed as Anglo-Saxon; an example is Stillingfleet (North Yorkshire), which has a representation of a very Viking-looking longship with a dragon's head prow (fig. 20).

4
Constructional elements

Certain constructional features are particularly common in Anglo-Saxon buildings, though none is universal. Tall narrow walls, distinctive quoining, the use of pilaster strips and hood-moulds and certain types of door and window arches are the main touchstones of recognition.

Walling was normally constructed of locally available materials, whether of stone or wood, though petrological examination of the reused stones of Brixworth church (Northamptonshire) suggests that they might have been used originally in Roman Leicester, which is nearly 30 miles (48 km) away. In some instances, it appears that wooden walls rested upon stone foundation courses, as with the rather flimsy footings for the north porticus at Escomb (Durham). Foundations could be of dry stone or clay-bonded or mortared below ground, but above ground stone and mortar were most commonly used. The quality of walling depended upon the materials available and the status of the building. It varies from dressed ashlar blocks at sites like Bradford-on-Avon (Wiltshire) to coursed rubblework, herringbone fabric, as in the upper parts of the nave at Deerhurst St Mary's (Gloucestershire), and random rubble. There seem to be no obvious reasons why one technique was preferred over another, but as exterior plastering was apparently fairly usual this is perhaps unsurprising. As further detailed examinations of churches takes place, reports of plinths at the bottoms of walls are proving more common.

Angles were normally tied in with quoins of five types: side-alternate, face-alternate, long-and-short, rubble and random megalithic; long-and-short quoins are perhaps the most distinctive (fig. 21). The origins of long-and-short quoins are obscure, but the absence of clear continental analogues argues strongly for an insular origin. A further feature of the angles of some later Saxon buildings is the use of *entasis*. This technique, which was invented by the ancient Greeks, is used to correct the illusion of concavity resulting from vertical walls; it is clearly illustrated at Wittering (Cambridgeshire, fig. 22) and Odda's Chapel at Deerhurst. It appears as an even tapering inwards of the angles of a structure, an effect too controlled to be fortuitous.

Door and window openings are normally round-headed, though a few triangular-headed openings appear in later build-

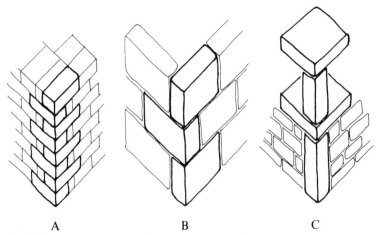

A   B   C

Fig. 21. Different types of quoins. **A** Face-alternate. **B** Side-alternate. **C** Long-and-short.

ings, notably at Deerhurst (fig. 23e), where there are triangular-headed double windows and a triangular-headed door in the nave. Circular lights are known at Bibury (Gloucestershire) and Hales (Norfolk); at Hales the circular window in the Saxo-Norman tower retains its original basketwork keying for the internal plastering (fig. 24, bottom). The heads of openings were either cut from single blocks of stone, as at Escomb (fig. 24, top) or were formed of irregular voussoirs, normally without a distinct keystone. At Corhampton (Hampshire), however, a regular keystone is advanced to form an effective architectural focus in the chancel arch before the sanctuary. In the very late Saxon western tower at St Mary-le-Wigford (Lincoln) the double belfry lights also have narrow keystones (fig. 23h). Doorways are often tall and narrow, and the proportions could on occasion become extreme, as at Ledsham (West Yorkshire), where a doorway only 2 feet (0.6 m) wide rises to a height of 14 feet (4.3 m).

Early windows tend to be single-splayed (fig. 23a), but later some were double-splayed both inside and out, presumably to admit more light. Some single-splayed windows appear to have been recut later in the new style, as at Bradford-on-Avon (fig. 23c). During the later Saxon period, when western towers became more common, double belfry openings with mid-wall shafts appear. The central shaft of these lights normally supports a 'through-stone' from which the heads of the openings spring in turn (fig. 23i). Certain types of windows show local variation: in

Fig. 22. East end of Wittering church showing fine long-and-short quoins rebated to take plaster.

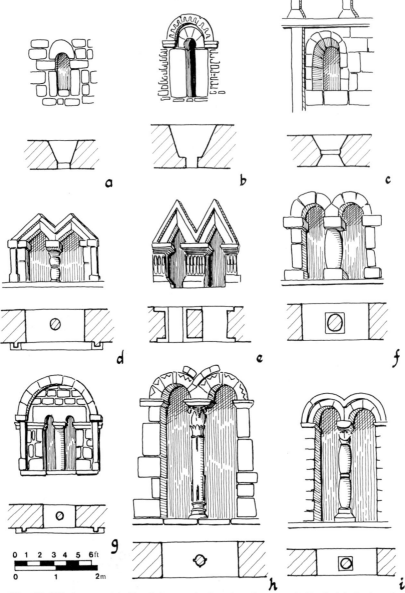

Fig. 23. Windows and belfry lights: **a** single splay, Jarrow; **b** 'keyhole' single splay, Glentworth (Lincolnshire); **c** double splay, Bradford-on-Avon; **d** mid-wall shaft with triangular heads, Barton-upon-Humber; **e** triangular-headed double windows, Deerhurst; **f** double window with mid-wall shaft, Worth; **g** Northumbrian belfry lights with stripwork surround, Monkwearmouth; **h** mid-wall shaft with decorated capital, St Mary-le-Wigford, Lincoln; **i** double belfry light with mid-wall shaft, Barton-upon-Humber.

Fig. 24. *(Top)* Window with monolithic head, Escomb. *(Bottom)* Blocked circular window showing basketwork keying for plaster, Hales (Norfolk).

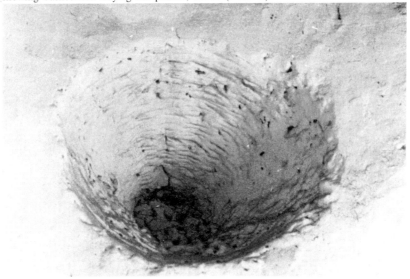

Fig. 25. Doors: *(top left)* main south doorway into Barnack tower with ornate stripwork; *(top right)* north door into the tower at Barton-upon-Humber; *(bottom left)* west tower door at Rothwell with a plain tympanum; *(bottom right)* a very late Saxon door showing clear Norman influence in its strong roll mouldings, at Hovingham (North Yorkshire).

Lincolnshire, for example, we find 'keyhole' windows (fig. 23b) and in Northumberland some tower lights were outlined in stripwork (fig. 23g). Wooden window frames survive at some sites, and the vertical grooves for wooden shutters can be seen on the nave windows at Escomb.

Greater arches tend to narrowness like the doorways, and they usually have a single square order round the head. Hoodmould-ings are fairly common (fig. 25, top left), often occurring as simple stripwork concentric with the head of the arch. Jambs may be formed in a variety of ways, including the use of very large through-stones set horizontally and vertically in 'Escomb fashion', a technique which echoes the long-and-short quoins.

The general simplicity of the arches extends to the imposts, and most are square in section and plan. Occasionally, as at Barnack (Cambridgeshire, fig. 27, left), stepped profiles occur, and even more rarely they are decorated with freestyle carving; beasties are particularly favoured and occur at Selham (Hampshire), Netheravon (Wiltshire, fig. 27, right) and St Benet's church at Cambridge. Capitals usually display variations on a basic scheme of a cube resting on a sphere or cone shape (fig. 26) and have a very functional appearance. Some of the most advanced capitals occur at Great Paxton (Cambridgeshire) above quarter-engaged cylindrical shafts; they are somewhat bulbous in form and have small foliate fillets (fig. 26j). The design of the Paxton capitals, as with some other late Saxon sites, prefigures Romanesque cushion capitals, but this need imply no more than insular development (fig. 26c).

String courses occur widely on both internal and external surfaces and are usually made of stone, though at Colchester Holy Trinity they are formed of clay tiles. One of the earliest examples occurs on the western porch at Monkwearmouth (Tyne and Wear), presumably constructed by Benedict Biscop's Gaulish masons. Whether or not the string course was introduced from Gaul, it became a familiar and distinctive feature of English architecture. Internally, string courses are often carried round door heads and other openings as hoodmouldings. Simple square sections are most common, though at Barnack (Cambridgeshire) and Breedon-on-the-Hill (Leicestershire, fig. 30g) they are elaborately carved. The Barnack example runs into the complex impost of the tower arch shown in fig. 27 and bears similar decoration. Externally, string courses were used to punctuate otherwise featureless towers, as at Rothwell (Lincolnshire, fig. 10, top left). Since they occur high up on many towers, it is

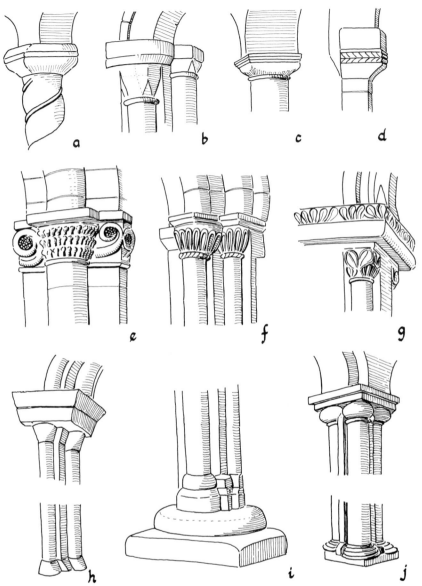

Fig. 26. Imposts, capitals and bases: **a** spiral decorated column with simple capital (Repton crypt); **b** impost of tower arch, Broughton by Brigg (Humberside); **c** shallow cushion capital from nave arcade at Ickleton (Cambridgeshire); **d** impost of north door at Daglingworth (Gloucestershire) with 'wheat ear' motif; **e** elaborate impost of tower arch at Sompting; **f** a very late tower arch bearing palmette decoration, Carlton-in-Lindrick (Nottinghamshire); **g** an example of debased palmette ornament from Hadstock (Essex); **h** impost and base of massive chancel arch at Wittering; **i** base of chancel arch at Bosham; **j** capital and base of the remarkable four-shaft nave arcade at Great Paxton.

possible that they also fulfilled the practical function of helping to shed water from the wall faces. This suggestion is based on the known water-shedding properties of hoodmouldings round openings. At Earls Barton (Northamptonshire) and Barton-upon-Humber (Humberside) string courses form an integral part of elaborate stripwork schemes. This suggests that they were also regarded as a decorative medium in their own right, since the designs at both sites exceed any strictly practical requirements. That string courses could be used as vehicles for decoration is clear from the examples cited above.

Mention of Earls Barton and Barton-upon-Humber inevitably leads to the question of vertical pilaster strips. As with the string course, it seems possible that they were a continental and ultimately classically inspired idea, but they were developed to great effect by the Anglo-Saxons. A variety of foreign parallels has been suggested for the pilaster strip, notably the early ninth-century 'tower gateway' into the monastery of St Nazarius at Lorsch (West Germany). But whilst Carolingian influences might be expected to make themselves felt in England at that time, none of the foreign parallels are really close. The lack of 'Lombard bands' of small blind arches in England which were *de rigeur* in the Ottonian period suggests that contacts were not important then either. Perhaps it is best to be persuaded by the occurrence of curved and diagonal members at Earls Barton in particular (fig. 28) that the work is redolent of the timber construction which was the Anglo-Saxons' stock-in-trade and hence was a native development.

As the strips often occur with rubble walling, it has been suggested that they assisted the builders to 'true up' the wall faces and that they would have helped to limit structural failure once

Fig. 27. Imposts: *(left)* north impost of tower arch at Barnack; *(right)* north impost of western tower entrance, Netheravon.

the wall was built. These explanations seem plausible enough, but the comparative rarity of the strips suggests that their structural value was not appreciated by all Anglo-Saxon builders. Also, their use at Bradford-on-Avon and Milborne Port (Dorset) in conjunction with good ashlar work permits no such practical explanation.

Whilst the strips may originally have had a practical purpose, it appears that this rapidly became secondary to their decorative value at several sites; certainly the complexity of the schemes at Earls Barton and Barton-upon-Humber suggests more *joie d'esprit* than practicality. The deep penetration of pilaster strips into the wall fabric (up to a foot at Deerhurst) has encouraged the 'functionalist' interpreters, but as the stones making up the strips can be several feet in length, considerable countersinking would be required simply to ensure that they did not fall out.

Fig. 28 *(left)*. Earls Barton tower from the south-west. As with virtually all Anglo-Saxon towers, the topmost stage (battlemented here) is a later addition; perhaps this means that the original towers had wooden tops which have not survived.

Fig. 29. The Great Rood at Romsey. Note the very large stones used in its construction; the original is about life-size.

5
Architectural decoration

Although not widely known, a considerable body of Anglo-Saxon architectural sculpture has survived, and it must serve as an imperfect indication of the richness of the early churches. The general absence of paint on the surviving material robs us of the vital dimension of colour; most sculpture was brightly, even gaudily painted. Much of the decoration occurs on the structural elements such as the capitals, imposts and bases described in chapter 4 (figs. 23 and 26). To these can be added roods, sundials, carved panels of various sorts, tympana, animal heads and occasional furnishings such as stone chairs and fonts.

Roods, which are representations of the Crucifixion, are particularly common in the south of England and were often carved at about life-size. At Headbourne Worthy (Hampshire) a mutilated example can be seen *in situ* above the west door. Similarly at Breamore (Hampshire) a rood is prominently sited above the principal south entrance to the minster church. At Romsey (Hampshire) an intact rood is built into the later abbey church; the Hand of God is shown as a symbol of authority above Our Lord's head (fig. 29). This motif is repeated in the small carved panel of the Virgin and Child at Inglesham (Wiltshire). The carved flying angels at Bradford-on-Avon (Wiltshire) and at Winterbourne Steepleton (Dorset) were probably originally associated with roods. Similarly at Bibury (Gloucestershire) traces of standing figures, probably St Mary and St John, to each side of the position occupied by the rood above the chancel arch attest some larger scheme. Smaller versions of the subject are known, the rustic panel at Daglingworth (Gloucestershire) being a good example. The lesser rood at Romsey features two angels above the cross, though there they are standing rather than flying. Where large roods survive *in situ*, they are generally fixed over the main entrance to a church or above the chancel arch. In either position they would have evoked the reverence which their majestic scale and sombre subject matter demanded.

Sundials occur quite widely in Anglo-Saxon churches and were normally built into the south wall. Time keeping must have been difficult and such sundials would have been essential for the regulation of services, particularly as church bells appear to have been uncommon before late Saxon times. Most are fairly straightforward with a gnomon at the centre of a squared block

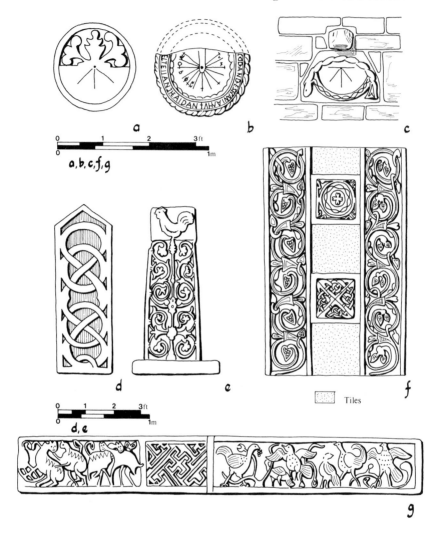

Fig. 30. Sundials and carved panels: **a** Barnack; **b** Orpington; **c** Escomb; note the projecting animal head above; **d** pierced screen from the belfry stage of Barnack tower; **e** decorated slab, Barnack; **f** remarkable lining of the porticus arch at Britford; **g** decorated friezework from Breedon-on-the-Hill.

Fig. 31. Carved figure panels: **a** the 'Breedon Angel'; **b** the Harrowing of Hell, Bristol Cathedral; note how Christ tramples the sinners underfoot and raises the good to Heaven; **c** a rustic Christ in Majesty from Daglingworth; **d** a much more accomplished, though rather foreign version, from Barnack. (Not to scale.)

| 0 | 1 | 2 | 3ft |

| 0 | | | 1m |

Fig. 32. Hoveringham tympanum: St Michael fights the dragon whilst the Agnes Dei looks on from the left.

with three or more radiating lines below marking the 'tides'. At Barnack (Cambridgeshire, fig. 30a) and in the Hampshire group around Winchester, foliate decoration was added to this basic pattern, and at Escomb (Durham, fig. 30c) a serpent curled around the dial might signify Eternity. At Kirkdale (North Yorkshire) a fine example is set in a rectangular panel with an inscription indicating 'This is the day's sun-marking at every hour'. Also recorded is the fact that Orm, son of Gamal, rebuilt the church in 'the days of Edward the King and Tosti the Earl' (of Northumbria), which fixes the date with unusual precision to the decade 1055-65. Perhaps the finest of these sundials was found during the restoration of All Saints church at Orpington (Greater London). This had fine cable moulding about its circumference with an Anglo-Saxon inscription set concentrically within it. On the face are sixteen tide lines and what was probably the Latin word *ORLOGIUM* carved about its top, of which only the first and last pairs of letters survive (fig. 30b).

Carved panels exist in many forms and some, such as the pierced examples in the belfry at Barnack (fig. 30d), were functional, in that case to permit the passage of sound. Other functional slabs include pieces of stone altar screens at South Kyme (Lincolnshire), Hexham (Northumberland) and Bradford-on-Avon. At Britford (Wiltshire) the jambs of the doorway into the north porticus bear a unique scheme of panelled decoration (fig. 30f), a constructional technique which was also used on the door into the porticus at Reculver (Kent). Most carved panels were purely decorative however, and their iconography was doubtless intended to concentrate the minds of the lay congregation on particular aspects of the faith: the Harrowing of Hell slab in Bristol Cathedral (fig. 31b) is a powerful example of such an image, and to this can be added the angel of Breedon-on-the-Hill (Leicestershire, fig. 31a) and the very different renderings of Christ in Majesty at Barnack and Daglingworth (fig. 31c and d).

Even the extensive use of vinescroll ornament was not without significance; in *John* XV, 5, Christ said 'I am the vine, and you are the branches,' and the Cross was viewed as a symbol of the regeneration of the church, which was itself like a vine (fig. 30f). At Edenham (Lincolnshire) a rare external scheme includes foliate roundels, and at Barnack three large foliate slabs are built into the external walls of the tower (fig. 30e). At Breedon-on-the-Hill a rich assemblage of friezework (fig. 30g) and figure panels, of which the Breedon angel (fig. 31a) is the most impressive, attests the magnificence and variety of the effects which Anglo-Saxon sculptors could achieve. Some of the friezework at Breedon may be *in situ,* and it probably ran all round the interior and exterior of the building.

The dating of the relatively small number of decorated tympana which survive from the pre-Conquest period has been hotly disputed; some have even claimed that all are Norman. Whilst many undoubtedly Norman tympana exhibit strong Anglo-Saxon influence, a few are generally accepted as being late Saxon. At Castor (Cambridgeshire) a reused example depicting Christ in Majesty has been dated as early as the ninth century. A very different type of scheme, featuring elaborate interlaced animals, at Knook (Wiltshire) has been plausibly likened to manuscript art of the tenth century and may well be of that period. More difficult are 'overlap' works, such as that built into the north transept at Southwell (Nottinghamshire) and the handsome piece from Hoveringham in the same county (fig. 32). The Southwell carving of St Michael and the dragon is Anglo-Saxon in style, but the occurrence of the piece at 'Norman' Southwell has led some to doubt whether it is the only surviving fragment of the tenth-century minster church on the site.

At a few sites, notably Barnack and Deerhurst St Mary's (Gloucestershire) strange projecting animal heads are incorporated into the exterior wall faces. They often occur over window openings and at Barnack at least served a structural function as one is used as a corbel to support a pilaster strip. Elsewhere no such practical explanation is apparent, and they are perhaps best seen as barbarous decorations. The origins of these heads are unknown, though their superficial resemblance to Viking ship figureheads has led to erroneous conclusions that they were a Scandinavian innovation. Their occurrence as unsupported projections suggests that, like other elements of external decoration, they owe more to timber building technology than to masonry construction.

The early Northumbrian churches are particularly rich in fragments of stone furnishings and internal fittings. Apart from the altar screens *(cancellae)* mentioned earlier, supports for the arms of chairs and benches are attested, as well as turned stone baluster shafts which were used to subdivide internal spaces. The frithstool at Hexham is the best known of the Anglo-Saxon stone chairs, and to this can be added the rather battered throne at Norwich.

Of the claimed Anglo-Saxon fonts, only a few can be accepted with certainty. At Melbury Bubb (Dorset) and at Deerhurst the fonts appear to be made from lengths of reused cross shafts and, whilst the original pieces are undoubtedly Saxon, the date of their reuse is unknown. At Potterne (Wiltshire) and Little Billing (Northamptonshire) greater certainty is possible since both bear Latin inscriptions in what is perhaps a tenth-century style. Excavations at Potterne have revealed traces of a small timber chapel near the later stone church, and in a baptistry annexe was found a recess of the same size as the base of the font. It is possible that the very simple Saxon font at King's Sutton (Northamptonshire), which was dug up in the churchyard in 1923, was *in situ* in its original baptistry.

After having considered detailed aspects of architectural decoration, we will briefly turn to the broader scale. Most exteriors of Saxon buildings were probably plastered, and it is likely that they were either whitewashed or even painted in colour. At St Mary Bishophill Junior, York, however, recent detailed examination of the fabric of the tower has revealed that the external wall faces were ornamented by bands of differently coloured stones, a technique which is well known in later Romanesque buildings.

The decorative potentialities of stripwork schemes have been reviewed in chapter 4. Blind arcading is a decorative device which

Fig. 33. Wing church from the east showing the stripwork decorated polygonal apse.

is quite often found, notably at Bradford-on-Avon and Great Tey (Essex); variations on the basic theme of arcading occur at Great Dunham (Norfolk), where there are niches in the side walls of the tower, and in the shallow pilasters (fig. 12) on the round tower at Haddiscoe Thorpe in the same county. Arcading also occurs on the polygonal chancels at Deerhurst and Wing (Buckinghamshire, fig. 33). The triangular shapes in the upper parts of the chancel walls at Wing remind us of the delicate triangular-headed arcade set in the north wall of the nave at Geddington (Northamptonshire).

When we turn to interiors, the discovery that the paintings of angels in the nave of the church at Nether Wallop (Hampshire) are Anglo-Saxon has revolutionised our ideas about Anglo-Saxon decoration. They are superbly designed and executed and are clearly influenced by the Winchester School. They are dated to the tenth century. Let nobody underestimate the quality of

Anglo-Saxon interior finishes!

Sadly, there is comparatively little other evidence for interior decoration; much must have disappeared at the hands of later 'restorers'. At Great Dunham there exists a somewhat mutilated scheme of internal decoration which includes delicately wrought blank arcading. From the excavations at the Old Minster in Winchester come a fragment of a sculpted and painted slab and a piece of painted plaster, but all this is little enough to show. We must hope that other detailed examinations and excavations will swell the evidence in future.

Fig. 34. Harold's manor house at Bosham, as depicted on the Bayeux Tapestry.

6
Wooden buildings

Although this book is primarily concerned with stone buildings, most of which are churches, it should not be forgotten that wood was the principal constructional material of the Anglo-Saxons. The word *getimber*, the Anglo-Saxon 'to build', clearly reveals its associations. Wooden houses, palaces and even churches are well attested throughout the period, and stone building must always have been exceptional. The concentration here on stone building is more a reflection of the survival of the evidence than of any qualitative judgement. Surviving Scandinavian wooden churches slightly later than the Anglo-Saxon period demonstrate a high degree of skill in planning and execution. They are no less 'architectural' because they were made of wood.

Apart from a few manuscript illustrations, the Bayeux Tapestry (fig. 34) and oblique literary references, archaeology must be our principal source of evidence for wooden buildings. Excavation of timber buildings commonly reveals a more or less complex pattern of areas of discoloured soil where timbers have rotted *in situ*. Occasionally, as at West Stow (Suffolk), charred timbers are found which are better preserved; waterlogging will also ensure better survival.

The principal difficulty with the archaeological evidence for timber buildings is that it produces only two dimensions of the structures. Laymen and experts alike find it difficult to envisage an upstanding building from its plan alone, and this has blunted the appreciation of the sophistication of such buildings. If we contrast the relatively simple ground plan of the twelfth-century timber church at Borgund (Norway) (fig. 35) with its very elaborate superstructure, we get some idea of the implications of this. Unfortunately the only English example of a timber nave, at Greensted (Essex), is unprepossessing (fig. 36), though the quality of the Saxon carpentry inside the 'helm' roof at Sompting (West Sussex, fig. 19) partly redresses the balance.

At West Stow, the excavator of an Anglo-Saxon village, Mr Stanley West, has taken the unusual step of reconstructing some of the building types encountered (fig. 37). The results, though controversial in some respects, give a good impression of the smaller domestic architecture of the early Saxon period. The first category of buildings was small huts, which were apparently used as workshops, storehouses and sheds. These huts had the unusual

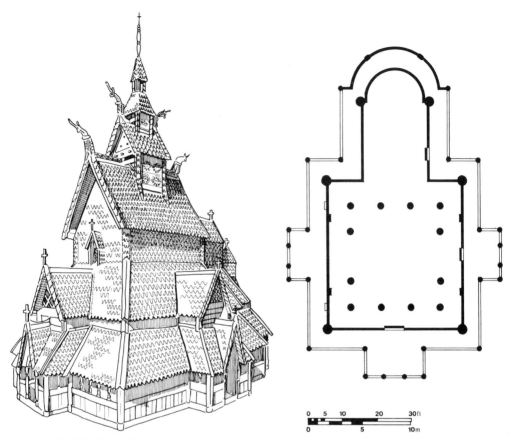

Fig. 35. The twelfth-century church at Borgund (Norway). Contrast the simplicity of its plan with the luxuriousness of its superstructure. (Plan after Bannister Fletcher.)

feature of a hole or air space beneath them, and some have claimed that the hut floors were countersunk into the ground. Others maintain that they were simply cellars or air spaces designed to overcome the problems of dampness under wooden floors. The West Stow huts are reconstructed with suspended wooden floors, and this seems more sensible than nasty damp 'pit dwellings'.

The second type of structure at West Stow is the 'hall'. Unlike the huts, which simply had postholes at each end, these larger buildings have walls composed of closely set vertical timbers. The halls are certainly more elaborate of construction, and Mr West has claimed them as dwellings by contrast with the huts which are ancillary buildings. The West Stow reconstructions are 'minimalist', and in the case of the halls in particular the quality of the original finishes would doubtless have been much higher.

The hall seems to have formed the basic unit at most Anglo-

Fig. 36. The massive timbers of the nave at Greensted. (Photograph by Peter Warner.)

Fig. 37. *(Top)* Reconstructed huts at West Stow Heath. *(Bottom)* Reconstructed hall at West Stow. (Photograph by Peter Warner.)

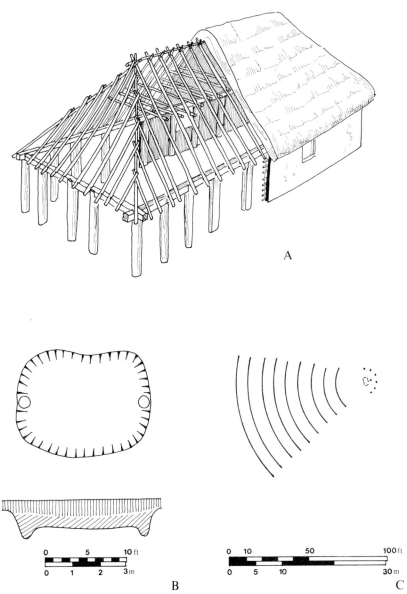

Fig. 38. A Reconstructed hall at Chalton with posts in individual postholes (after R. Warmington). **B** Plan and section of sunken floored hut from West Stow (after West). **C** Plan of 'grandstand' at Yeavering (after Colvin).

Saxon settlements, irrespective of status. At Chalton (Hampshire, fig. 38) and Catholme (Staffordshire) village excavations have yielded many such, whilst at Sulgrave (Northamptonshire) and Portchester (Hampshire) later Saxon aristocratic examples have been located. Higher status is generally reflected by somewhat larger buildings with subsidiary structures grouped about them. A similar pattern, though on a yet larger scale, is observable at the royal palace sites at Yeavering (Northumberland) and Cheddar (Somerset). At these sites the main halls are very substantial, and we can imagine that their fabric and finish were of the highest quality, as became their royal status.

A remarkable feature of the palace site at Yeavering, probably the place called 'ad Gefrin' by Bede, was the existence of an assembly place or 'grandstand'. This structure, which resembles a section of a Roman theatre, is unparalleled elsewhere and might represent the council-place of the kings of Northumbria (fig. 38C). If this site was ad Gefrin, it is possible that St Paulinus preached to the Northumbrian nobility whilst they sat on this grandstand during his recorded visit to the site in 627.

Paulinus belonged to the Celtic church which, in England at least, appears to have built almost exclusively in wood. Literary evidence suggests that even the churches of major Celtic monastic sites like Lindisfarne and Glastonbury were made of wood, and this implies that the subsidiary structures would have been similarly constructed. This is in sharp contrast with the monastic churches of the Latin mission, which were built of brick and stone from the first. The new building technology represented by such sites as Monkwearmouth and Jarrow was the outward and visible sign of the rift between the two churches which culminated in the Synod of Whitby in 663. If the Roman party had not triumphed over the Celtic on that occasion stone architecture might not have become fashionable in Anglo-Saxon England. Certainly the evidence of secular buildings suggests it would not have done.

It should not be thought that all churches were built in stone after the Synod of Whitby, however. Wooden churches must always have been common, and the sole survivor at Greensted was perhaps built as late as the eleventh century. Excavations at Rivenhall (Essex) and Wharram Percy (North Yorkshire) have revealed the fragmentary remains of timber churches which were themselves replaced in stone during the Saxon period. This pattern must have been very common, with timber being replaced by stone as funds permitted. On the continent, where the excavation of church sites is more common, the transition from wood to stone is well known, and it is the relative paucity of such investigations in England which has unbalanced the evidence of wooden churches.

7
Recent research

There has recently been a tremendous increase in interest in Anglo-Saxon archaeology generally and in architecture in particular. Major research projects with a multi-disciplinary basis, bringing together the skills of historians, archaeologists and architectural historians, show one important way forward. At Brixworth, Deerhurst, Barton-upon-Humber and Repton this type of approach has yielded most encouraging results and is yet continuing. Also, the careful observation of alterations to existing churches has led to surprising discoveries, notably at Rivenhall (Essex), where a seemingly Victorian church proved to be very largely of Anglo-Saxon date once the plaster was removed from the walls. So many discoveries have been made recently that a great deal of new information has become available.

Not all the recent work has been directed towards major buildings, and the lesser churches of town and country have fared well. At Gloucester, Lincoln, Thetford, Winchester and Cirencester, to name but a few examples, important new discoveries of churches have been made. It is to be hoped that early churches will continue to enjoy a high priority in urban excavation programmes. Similarly in the countryside, at Raunds (Northamptonshire) and Wharram Percy (North Yorkshire), evidence for the vital early stages of church development has been found. Fortunately, the Medieval Village Research Group, which advises the Department of the Environment on research priorities, recommends further elucidation of Saxon village sites, including their churches.

More detailed surveys of documentary sources for the appearance and function of Saxon buildings are being undertaken, and some earlier theories are being reviewed. In parallel with this, studies of architectural details such as capitals, imposts and sculpture will help to highlight regional and local styles as well as the chronology of the difficult 'Saxo-Norman' phase. Tree-ring dating has been used to some effect on Saxon timber scaffold poles found embedded in walls and, as this technique improves, we might expect great assistance with at least the broad chronology.

8
Sites to visit

There are four hundred or so churches which have some Anglo-Saxon fabric, but the following is a list of some of the more rewarding sites to visit. All these and more sites are contained in the book *A Guide to Anglo-Saxon Sites* by Nigel and Mary Kerr (Granada).

Barnack (Cambridgeshire). Tower of church, parts of nave, sculpture and stone quarries.

Barton-upon-Humber (Humberside). Tower nave church.

Bibury (Gloucestershire). Damaged rood, circular windows.

Bosham (West Sussex). Late and advanced Saxon church.

Bradford-on-Avon (Wiltshire). The controversial chapel of St Laurence.

Bradwell-on-Sea (Essex). Upstanding nave of St Cedd's church.

Breamore (Hampshire). Minster church with important inscription.

Breedon-on-the-Hill (Leicestershire). Large quantity of excellent sculpture from the early monastery.

Britford (Wiltshire). Unique carved panels.

Brixworth (Northamptonshire). Imposing basilican church with later Saxon ring crypt and tower.

Bywell (Northumberland). Two Saxon churches in one small village; one has a Northumbrian Group tower.

Cambridge, St Benet's church. Fine tower arch and traces of original 'helmed' roof.

Canterbury (Kent). Shrine of Christendom with major early churches.

Carlton-in-Lindrick (Nottinghamshire). Very late Saxon tower with herringbone work.

Daglingworth (Gloucestershire). Rustic carved slabs.

Deerhurst (Gloucestershire). The monastic church of St Mary and Odda's Chapel.

Earls Barton (Northamptonshire). Stripwork decorated tower.

Edenham (Lincolnshire). External decorative scheme.

Escomb (Durham). Seventh-century church, little altered.

Great Dunham (Norfolk). Internal decoration.

Great Paxton (Cambridgeshire). Late and advanced minster church.

Greensted (Essex). Timber nave.

Haddiscoe (Norfolk). Late Saxon round tower.

Hexham (Northumberland). Wilfrid's crypt and sculpture.

Hough-on-the-Hill (Lincolnshire). Tower with stair turret.

Jarrow (Tyne and Wear). Parts of monastic church and site museum.

Kirkdale (North Yorkshire). Late Saxon church and important sundial.

Knook (Wiltshire). Tympanum.

Langford (Oxfordshire). Roods and tower.

Ledsham (West Yorkshire). Early nave with later Saxon additions.

Lincoln. Late Saxon Lincolnshire Group towers at St Mary-le-Wigford and St Peter's church.

Melbury Bubb (Dorset). Font.

Milborne Port (Somerset). Saxon chancel and crossing.

Monkwearmouth (Tyne and Wear). Porch, tower and sculpture.

North Elmham (Norfolk). Saxon cathedral.

Orpington (Greater London). Sundial.

Reculver (Kent). Early church of Kentish Group.

Repton (Derbyshire). Crypt and parts of church.

Ripon (North Yorkshire). St Wilfrid's crypt.

Romsey (Hampshire). The greater and lesser roods.

Rothwell (Lincolnshire). Lincolnshire Group tower.

Sompting (West Sussex). 'Helmed' tower roof and sculpture.

Southwell (Nottinghamshire). Tympanum.

Stillingfleet (North Yorkshire). Door furniture.

Stow (Lincolnshire). Major late Saxon church.

West Stow (Suffolk). Early Saxon building reconstructions.

Wing (Buckinghamshire). Crypt and nave.

Wittering (Cambridgeshire). Two-cell church.

Worth (West Sussex). Fine apsidal church, although restored.

York. The enigmatic Anglian Tower behind the City Library.

9
Further reading

Most information regarding Anglo-Saxon architecture is to be found in articles in learned journals like *Medieval Archaeology* and the *Journal of the British Archaeological Association*. Rather than giving references to such sources, a few titles are suggested which will provide an introduction for the general reader which he can then pursue as desired.

Clapham, A. W. *English Romanesque Architecture* volume I. Oxford, 1930.

Taylor, H. M. and J. *Anglo-Saxon Architecture.* Cambridge, 1965.

Taylor, H. M. *Anglo-Saxon Architecture* volume III. Cambridge, 1978.

Wilson, D. M. *The Anglo-Saxons.* Penguin, 1972.

Wilson, D. M. (editor). *The Archaeology of Anglo-Saxon England.* Methuen, 1976.

10
Glossary

Aisle: division of a church normally running parallel to the nave, and divided from it by an arcade.

Ambulatory: an aisle enclosing an apse or straight-ended sanctuary, often used for processional purposes.

Apse: a semicircular termination of a chapel or chancel.

Arcade: row of arches on pillars or columns.

Ashlar: masonry constructed of square hewn stones.

Baluster: a short pillar often found at the centre of a two-light window.

Basilica: originally a Roman word which described a building divided into a nave and two or more aisles, the nave being higher and wider than the aisles to each side. This basic form was used for early Christian churches in the Mediterranean and can be seen in England at Hexham, Brixworth and elsewhere.

Batter: the inclined face of a wall, normally at the base.

Capital: the head of a column, often enriched with moulded decoration.

Carolingian: a dynasty of the Franks named after Charlemagne (742-814). It lasted until the death of Louis V in 987. During this period there was a classical revival, and Carolingian art and architecture reflected Roman models.

Celtic: a general term for the peoples and cultures of Cornwall, Wales, north-western England and the rest of the British Isles outside Anglo-Saxon England.

Chamfer: surface produced by cutting away the sharp edge of a stone block, normally at an angle of 45 degrees to the other planes.

Chancel: the east end of a church, which is reserved for the choir and clergy and the main altar.

Clerestory: the upper stage of the main walls of a church above the aisle roofs, pierced by windows.

Crypt: underground room beneath a church, often used for burials and the display of relics.

Entasis: slight convex curve used on columns and quoins to correct the optical illusion of concavity which would result if the sides were straight.

Foliate: leaf-like.

Franks: Germanic confederacy of small tribes which conquered France during the sixth century.

Freestone: any stone that cuts well in all directions, especially fine-grained limestone or sandstone.

Frieze: a decorative band of carving set into the surface of a wall.

Gnomon: rod or pin at the centre of a sundial which shows the time by casting its shadow on a marked surface.

Greek key decoration: a geometrical ornament of vertical and horizontal straight lines repeated to form a band.

Herringbone work: type of walling in which the stones are laid diagonally rather than horizontally. Alternate courses lie in opposite directions, forming a zigzag or 'herringbone' pattern on the wall face.

Hogback: tombstone in the form of a stylised house, the roof ridge of which has a 'hogback' shape, being higher at the centre than at the ends.

Impost: bracket set into a wall upon which the end of an arch rests.

Interlace: a pattern formed by intertwining one or more ribbons.

Jamb: the straight side of an archway, door or window.

Lintel: horizontal stone over a door or window opening.

Megalith: large stone.

Minster: mother church (not necessarily a cathedral or monastery) serving an area eventually divided up into parishes.

Monolith: a single stone.

Narthex: a chamber at the west end of a church sometimes used as a porch.

Nave: the western arm of a church, which normally forms the main body of the structure.

Oratory: small chapel used for private worship.

Order: on a doorway or a window, a series of concentric steps receding towards the opening.

Pilaster: shallow rectangular column projecting only slightly from a wall.

Plinth: the projecting base of a wall or column pedestal, generally chamfered or moulded on the top.

Porticus (singular and plural): these were side chapels built against the main walls of a church. Many were used for burials, since the burial of the dead was originally forbidden within the main body of a church.

Precinct: a reserved space round a monastic settlement, normally divided from the outside world by a wall or ditch.

Quoins: the squared stones at the corner of a building (fig. 21).

Reeding: decoration composed of parallel convex mouldings touching one another.

Relic: a revered object associated with a saint.

Reredos: a wall or screen set behind an altar and normally decorated.

Rood: this simply means a crucifix but also refers to the elaborate stone carvings of the Crucifixion which depict figures of the Virgin Mary and others.

Rotunda: building of circular ground plan, often with a dome.

Rubblework: rough unhewn building stones or flints, generally not laid in regular courses.

Soffit: the underside of an arch.

Spandrel: the triangular space between the side of an arch and its frame.

Splay: a sloping, chamfered surface cut into a wall. The term refers to the widening of doorways and windows by slanting the sides.

String course: a continuous projecting horizontal band set into the surface of a wall, sometimes decorated.

Stripwork: narrow lines of decorative stonework, often used to outline windows and doors.

Synod: an ecclesiastical council or meeting.

Transept: the transverse arms of a cross-shaped church, normally between nave and chancel.

Tympanum: space between the lintel of a door and the arch above it; often decorated.

Voussoir: a wedge-shaped stone used in the head of an arch.

Index